How to

Make and fly kites

Eve Barwell and Conrad Bailey

CRESCENT BOOKS, NEW YORK

Acknowledgments
The authors would like to thank all those friends,
amongst them Gary and Denise Wingrove, who helped
test fly the kites in this book.

Contents

How to choose your materials

Most of the materials used to make the kites in this book may be found around the house. Choose covers and sticks that weigh as little as possible. The lighter the kite, the better it will fly.

Covers
Most kites have a cloth or paper cover but you can experiment with other materials. Whatever you choose, the wind must not be able to blow through it. Suitable materials are:

paper :	brown paper
	crêpe paper
	fancy wrapping paper
	imitation Japanese paper (from a shop selling artists' materials)
	newspaper
	shelf paper
	tissue paper
	wallpaper
fabric :	artificial silk
	closely woven cotton
	lining materials
	silk
other things :	colored plastic sacks
	plastic wrapping materials (polyethylene, Saran Wrap, etc.)
	polystyrene tiles

Glue
All-purpose household glues will stick most of the materials mentioned in this book.

If you are making a polystyrene kite, test your glue on it first. Some glues 'melt' polystyrene and it is best to use the recommended tile cement.

For sticking plastics, polyethylene and Saran Wrap it is quicker and easier to use Sellotape, Scotch tape, or a similar adhesive tape.

Sticks
Each stick must be evenly balanced as well as light. To test one, mark the center of the stick and balance it across a pencil held in your hand. If one end hangs lower than the other, shave a little of it away with a knife.

Suitable materials are:
balsa wood (from a crafts and hobbies shop)
batons or dowelling
bamboo canes (from a gardening shop. Split them lengthwise with a knife to make them lighter.)
garden sticks (gardening shop)
old umbrella spokes
sticks from trees and hedges

String or cord
Any thin string or nylon or terylene cord may be used for making kites.

Six steps in Kitemaking

How to bind and glue the sticks

Wherever two or more sticks cross they must be tied and glued together. This gives the kite a really firm framework.

Lay the sticks in position. Tie on a piece of string or cord.

Wind the cord around the join like this . . .

. . . then like this.

And then weave it around, over and under the sticks like this.

Cover the cord with dabs of glue. Leave it to dry.

How to frame the kite

Most kites need a frame of string or cord. It helps the kite keep its shape and makes a firm edge for the cover.

Cut a notch in the end of each stick like this.

Tie a piece of string to one of the sticks. Leave a fairly long end.

Keeping the string taut, take it across to the notch on the next stick and wind it around two or three times.

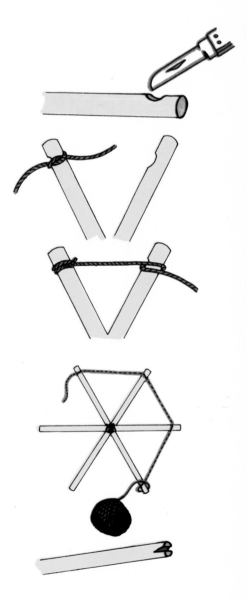

Wind the string around all the sticks in turn until you are back where you started. Tie the two ends of the string together.

(For the cutter kite on pages 20–21, cut the notches like this. Simply slot the string into the notches and pull it tight before you knot the two ends together.)

7

How to cover the kite

Lay the framework on the material you have chosen for the cover. Cut around it, cutting the cover larger than the frame all the way around.

Cut away the corners of the cover.

Bend the edges of the cover over the frame and stick them down with glue or adhesive tape.

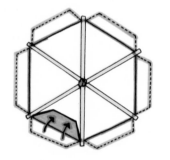

Cut little notches in any curved edges of the cover before gluing them down.

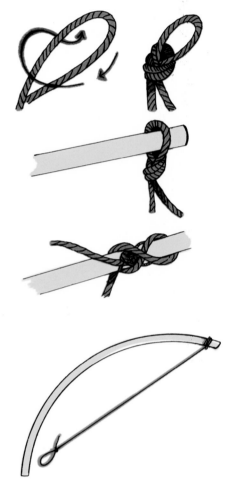

How to bow the kite

Many kites will fly better if they have a curved or bowed surface towards the wind instead of a flat one.

Cut a piece of string 6 in. (15 cm) longer than the stick you want to bow. Bend each end back 3 in. (7.5 cm) and knot them like this.*

Lay the kite face down and slip one of the loops over one end of the stick.

Stop the loop slipping along the stick by winding string around it in a figure eight.

Bend the stick gently until you can slip the other loop over the other end. Fasten it in position in the same way.

* These measurements are a useful guide for a medium-sized kite. For very large kites the string will have to be shorter than this (perhaps the same length as the stick) and for very small kites it will have to be longer.

9

How to make the bridle

The short strings from the ends of the sticks to the towing ring are called the bridle. They hold the kite at the correct angle to the wind while it is flying. A curtain ring makes a good towing ring.

Tie a piece of cord or string to the top of the spine. (The spine is the stick that goes from top to bottom of the kite.) The instructions for the individual kite will tell you how long that string should be.

Loop it two or three times through a curtain ring and tie it to the bottom of the spine. Slide the ring along the string until it is in the right place. (It will always be nearer the top of the kite than the bottom.)

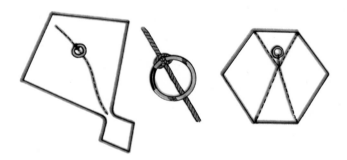

Some kites have a double bridle. This means they have another string tied to each end of one of the other sticks. This piece of string is looped through the curtain ring too.

When the ring is in the right position on the strings, wind a small piece of adhesive tape around the strings behind the ring to hold it firm.

How to make a tail

Almost every kind of kite needs a tail. Some need more than one. Often a tail has to be up to five times as long as the kite so as to help it balance properly. Make the tail from the same material as the kite.

Cut your paper, fabric or plastic into strips about 8 in. (20 cm) by 2 in. (5 cm). Tie the strips onto a long piece of string, spacing them about 8 in. (20 cm) apart. It will help if you anchor one end of the string to a door handle or chair leg before you start. Tie the finished tail to the bottom of the kite.

If your kite is small and very light you will need a very light tail. Try a paper tassel. Cut a long narrow strip of paper about 20 in. (50 cm) long and 4 in. (10 cm) wide. Cut a deep fringe in one of the long edges, then roll the paper up tightly. Bind the top with adhesive tape. Use a piece of string about the same length as the kite to tie the tassel to it.

Kites

Aero-kite

You need:
2 sticks the same length
1 stick about one third as long as the others
paper
string and curtain ring
glue, pencil and ruler

1 Use the pencil to mark the center of each of the three sticks. Divide one of the longer sticks in half again. Lay out the three sticks as in the diagram. Bind and glue them where they touch (see page 6).

2 Frame the sticks (see page 7), crossing the frame cords at point **a.**

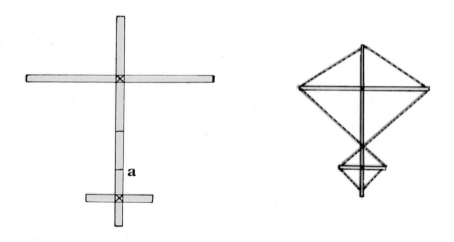

3 Cover the frame (see page 8). Snip the cover each side of point **a** so that the cover may be folded and glued down more easily.

4 Bow the wings and tail (see page 9).

Bridle (see page 10). Cut a piece of string a little longer than the wing section of the plane. Tie it to the top of the kite and point **a.**

Tail. This kite should fly without a tail.

Decoration. Paint the insignia of the air force or the initials of an airline onto the wings of the plane.

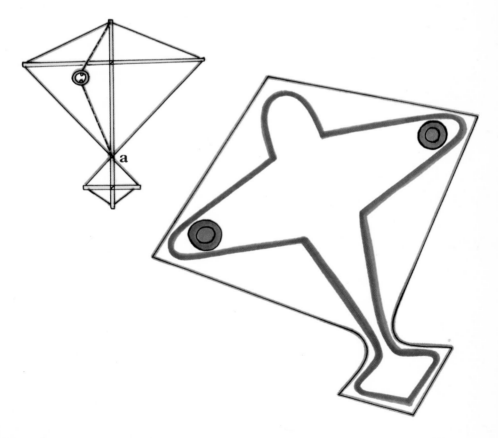

Bat

You need:
2 sticks the same length
a sheet of polyethylene,
    Saran Wrap or similar
    (large polyethylene
    bag)
glue, adhesive tape
black paper or felt-tipped
    pen
string and curtain ring
ruler and pencil
scissors

1 Mark the exact center of each stick. Divide one half of one of the sticks into two equal sections. Break off one of these sections and lay one stick across the other as shown in the diagram.

2 Bind and glue the sticks together (see page 6).

3 Lay the sticks on the polyethylene and use them as a guide for cutting the semi-circular shape. Fix the end of each stick to the polyethylene with a piece of adhesive tape.

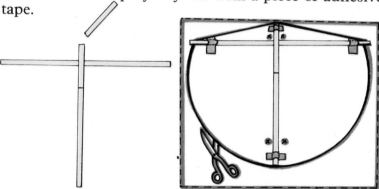

4 Bow the longer stick slightly (see page 9).

Bridle (see page 10). Cut a piece of string a little longer than the center stick. With the point of your pencil make small holes in the polyethylene at the points marked x. You will then be able to thread the string through the cover and tie it to the stick. The curtain ring should be about one quarter of the way along the string.

Decoration. Draw a bat on the polyethylene with a felt-tipped pen. (You may find it easier to draw the bat shape on thin black paper, cut it out, and stick it to the polyethylene with adhesive tape.)

This kite does not need a tail, Try flying it when it is getting dark. The Bat looks really eerie and sounds quite frightening as its plastic wings flap in the wind.

Bluebird

You need:
2 sticks the same length
1 flexible stick longer than
   the other two
a short firm piece of stick
paper and glue
string and curtain ring
paints, crayons or felt pens

1 Lay out the two identical sticks and the short firm piece in the shape of an 'A'. Bind and glue the sticks together where they touch (see page 6).

2 Lay the last stick across the A and bind and glue it in position.

3 Attach a string to point **b** and tie the other end to point **c** so that the cross stick is bent. Tie another string from **d** to **e**. Make sure that each wing is bent the same amount.

4 Cover the frame with paper (see page 8).

Bridles. Cut one piece of string to reach from **c** to **x** and back to **e**. Tie the ends to points **c** and **e**, looping the string through the curtain ring as you do so. Cut a second piece of string to reach from **c** to **x** and tie it to the tops of the wings at the points marked **y**, again remembering to loop it through the ring.

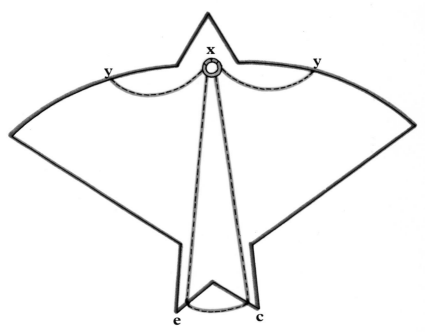

Tail (see page 11). Make a tail about three times the length of the kite. Tie a loop of string from **c** to **e** and hang the tail from it.

Decoration. Paint or draw the feathers onto your Bluebird.

Clown

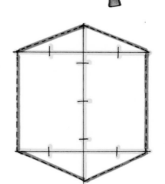

You need:
2 sticks the same length
1 stick about 5 in. (12 cm)
   longer
string, curtain ring
sheet of paper
glue
paints, pencil, ruler

1 Using the pencil and
ruler, divide each stick
into four equal parts.
Using the pencil marks as
guides, lay the shorter
sticks across the other one,
as shown in the diagram.

2 Bind and glue the sticks
together where they touch
(see page 6).

3 Frame the sticks with
cord or string (see page 7).

4 Cover the frame with
paper (see page 8).

5 Bow the two shorter
sticks (see page 9).

18

Bridle. Cut a piece of string long enough to reach from **a** to **x** and back to **a**. With the point of your pencil make a small hole in the cover each side of the stick at the two points marked **a**. Turn the kite over. Tie the ends of the string to the stick by threading them through the holes in the cover. Do not forget the curtain ring.

Cut a second piece of string to reach from **b** to **y** to **b**.

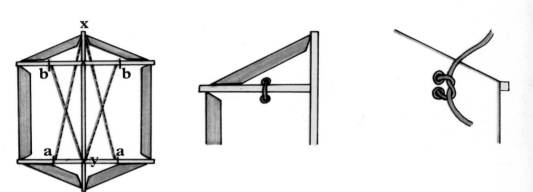

Make holes in the cover and tie the string to the points marked **b**. Slip the ring to the center of each piece of string.

Tail. Make a tail three times the length of the kite. Tie it to the bottom of the kite.

Decoration. Use paints or cut or torn paper to make the Clown's face. If you think the shape of the kite is more like a shield you may like to make up a coat of arms to paint on it instead.

Cutter kite

You need:
2 sticks the same length
knife
ruler, pencil
string, curtain ring
and either: a large sheet of paper
or: a large piece of fabric, needle and thread

1 Use the ruler and pencil to divide the sticks into equal parts. Lay the sticks across each other like this. Break off one third of one of the sticks.

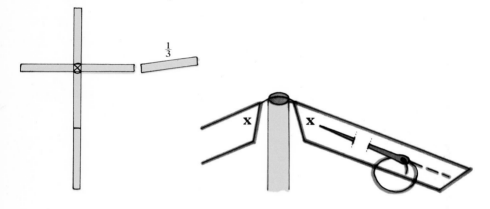

2 Bind and glue the sticks together where they touch (see page 6).

3 Make a string frame (see page 7 with the special note on cutter kites).

4 Cover the frame with paper or fabric (see page 8). If you use fabric you may still glue the edges over the frame, or you may sew it down using running stitches.

Bridles (see page 10). Cut a piece of string the length of one short and one long side of the kite. Tie it to the top and bottom. Cut a second piece the length of the two short sides of the kite and tie it to each side. Do not forget the curtain ring.

Tail (see page 11). Make a tail at least five times the length of the kite.

Variations. If you make a fabric Cutter, sew two long ribbons onto the cover at each corner at the points marked **x**. Tie each pair of ribbons together over the notch in the stick. This will help keep the cover in position and the ribbons will look pretty fluttering in the breeze.

If you wish, you can bow your kite (see page 9) to make it easier to fly.

You can also make a Cutter kite using three sticks instead of two, as shown in the two tiny diagrams at the top of the page.

Fish

You need:
3 sticks the same length
sheet of polyethylene,
   Saran Wrap or similar
scraps of tissue paper
string and curtain ring
adhesive tape
glue

1 Bind and glue the sticks together into the shape of a star (see page 6).

2 Make a string or cord frame (see page 7).

3 Cut a polyethylene cover for the frame (see page 8). Cut the cover extra wide between the top and bottom sticks so as to give your fish a more rounded shape.

Bridles (see page 10). Use two pieces of string. One should be long enough to reach from the two top sticks to the center of the kite (diagram **a**, opposite page). The other should reach from the two bottom sticks to a point half way between the center and the top of the kite (diagram **b**). The curtain ring should come in the center of both strings.

Tail. Make one about twice the length of the kite. Tie a loop of cord between the bottom two sticks and hang the tail from it.

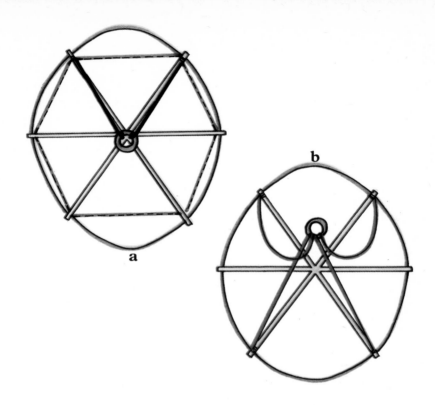

a

b

Decoration. Decorate with cut-out pieces of tissue paper glued to the cover. Some fish have stripes; some have spots. What kind of markings will yours have? Or will you give the kite a different face altogether?

Equipment you need for flying your kite

To fly a kite you need:

1 *a line*
String, nylon or terylene cord, or nylon fishing line are all suitable.

2 *pair of gloves*
Always wear gloves to prevent the line from cutting into your hands.

3 *extra tail*
This is a very useful thing to have with you. You will be surprised how often your kites need a longer or heavier tail than the one you have given them.

4 *clip*
If you have more than one kite and only one line, tie a clip from a dog's leash to the end of the line so that you can switch it easily from one towing ring to another.

5 *reel*
You can use a firm cardboard tube, or an old fishing reel, or make one of these designs in wood.

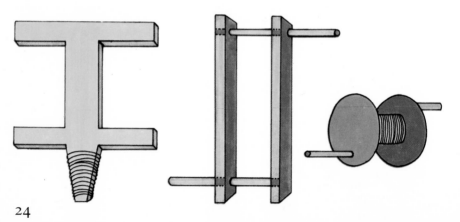

How to launch, fly and land your kite

Launching
Always stand with your back to the wind. Hold the kite by the towing ring at arm's length. The wind should simply lift it into the air, and it should not be necessary to run with the kite.

If you have a helper ask him to stand a little way in front of you, holding the kite tilted into the breeze. He should wait until the wind lifts the kite out of his hands and should never throw it into the air.

Flying
Do not let the line out too quickly once the kite is off the ground.

Help the kite to rise by pulling on the line. To do this, grip the line at arm's length. Bend your arm up and right back at the elbow, still gripping the line. Straighten your arm again slowly, at the same time letting the line slip through your fingers. Grip the line again and continue pulling and releasing it in this way until the kite is high enough in the sky.

If the kite slips slowly to the left, run across the breeze to the left. If it slips to the right, then run to the right.

If the kite dives suddenly to one side, quickly let out more line.

Adjusting
A flat kite should lean forward into the wind and fly at an angle of about 45°.

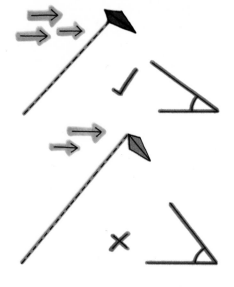

If your kite will not rise, perhaps it is flying too vertically. Move the towing ring nearer the top of the kite.

If your kite flutters, dips and thrashes about, perhaps it is flying too flat to the wind. Move the towing ring nearer the middle of the kite.

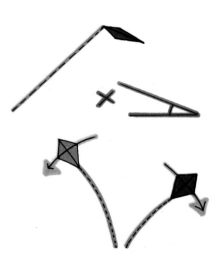

If your kite falls to the left, try moving the towing ring a little to the right. If it slips to the right, move the ring a little to the left.

If your kite dives, or spins, or loops the loop you must add a longer or heavier tail.

If the kite does not rise and the tail hangs down instead of streaming out behind, then you must shorten the tail.

Landing

Make sure there is no-one standing in front of you before you land your kite. Kites often crash when they come in low.

In a light breeze, simply wind in the line, In a stronger breeze, walk towards the kite as you wind in the line.

If you have a helper, ask him to hold the reel while you put your hand over the line and walk towards the kite, letting the line slip through your fingers. This will bring the kite down gradually.

Index